THE RAILROAD

Bobbie Kalman

🌱 Crabtree Publishing Company

www.crabtreebooks.com

LIFE IN THE OLD WEST

Created by Bobbie Kalman

With lots of love to my grandfather, J.P. Berube,
who worked for the railroad in days of yore

Author and Editor-in-Chief
Bobbie Kalman

Managing editor
Lynda Hale

Senior editor
April Fast

Project editor
Jane Lewis

Researcher
Amelinda Berube

Copy editors
Hannelore Sotzek
John Crossingham

Photo researcher
John Crossingham

Special thanks to
Mary Helmich, California State Parks;
California State Railroad Museum;
Joseph Pierre Berube

Computer design
Lynda Hale
Robert MacGregor (cover concept)
Campbell Creative Services

Production coordinator
Hannelore Sotzek

Crabtree Publishing Company

www.crabtreebooks.com   1-800-387-7650

In Canada: We acknowledge the financial support of the Government
of Canada for our publishing activities.

Printed in Canada/072018/MQ20180530

Library of Congress Cataloging in Publication Data
Kalman, Bobbie
   The railroad

(Life in the Old West)x
Includes index.

ISBN 0-7787-0076-3 (library bound) ISBN 0-7787-0108-5 (pbk.)
This book describes the development of the railroad in North America and its influence
on the settling of the West and the Native Americans during the nineteenth century.

1. Railroads—North America—History—19th century—Juvenile literature. 2. North
America—Economic conditions—19th century. [1. Railroads—West—North America—
History.] I. Title. II. Series: Kalman, Bobbie. Life in the Old West.

HE2751.K35 1999   j385'.0973   LC 99-11530
                                                                  CIP

Published in Canada
Crabtree Publishing
616 Welland Ave.
St. Catharines, ON
L2M 5V6

Published in the United States
Crabtree Publishing
PMB 59051
350 Fifth Avenue, 59th Floor
New York, New York 10118

Published in the United Kingdom
Crabtree Publishing
Maritime House
Basin Road North, Hove
BN41 1WR

Published in Australia
Crabtree Publishing
3 Charles Street
Coburg North
VIC, 3058

TABLE OF CONTENTS

THE JOURNEY WEST

In the early 1800s, travel in North America was slow and difficult. The best way to get from place to place was by boat. On land, there were few roads, and even short journeys to nearby cities or towns could take days. To reach faraway places, people had to cross wilderness areas with no bridges or mountain roads. Travel by horse and cart over uneven ground was uncomfortable and dangerous. People needed a better way to travel.

Heading west

The population in eastern North America was growing quickly, and cities were becoming busy and crowded. The government offered free land in the West to those who dared make the journey. The early settlers had to travel to the West by **wagon train**. The trip took months and involved crossing wide, deep rivers, dry prairie land, and difficult mountain passes. The settling of the West was very slow.

Changing travel and history

When the steam train was introduced as a quicker, safer way to travel, North America changed forever. Traveling by train was faster, more comfortable, and more convenient than any other form of transportation. It was also an affordable means of travel. People from all over the world could easily **emigrate** to the West to start a new life.

During its construction, the railroad provided countless people with work, and after the trains were running, people were needed to operate the trains and stations. Most important, the railroad contributed to the building of the United States and Canada as nations. It linked each country from coast to coast and took millions of settlers to their new homes and lives. The railroad played a big part in history.

EVOLUTION OF THE ENGINE

All early trains were operated by steam engines. The steam engine was invented in the 18th century and was used to power pumps that drained water out of underground mines. People soon thought of other uses for the steam engine. Inventors wondered whether it could be placed on wheels and used to pull carts. In the early 1800s, the first steam-powered engine, or **locomotive**, was built.

The iron horse

The first locomotives were only experiments. Many people doubted that steam engines would ever be powerful enough to be useful. They even set up a race between a locomotive and a horse in order to prove that a steam engine was not as fast as a horse. The horse won the race, but only because the locomotive broke down halfway along the track.

Some business people who saw the race realized how powerful the steam engine could be. They put time and money into developing a better locomotive. Eventually, steam engines replaced horses, pulling carts full of goods and people from place to place. The locomotive became known as "the iron horse."

(above) Richard Trevithick built the first steam-powered locomotive in England in 1804. Trevithick's engine was never used to pull a train, but it inspired other people to improve upon his invention.

(right) The DeWitt Clinton locomotive was one of the first American locomotives. It was built in 1831.

Over time, engines became larger and more powerful. Better engine designs allowed trains to travel at faster speeds and pull more weight. The American-style locomotive, shown above, was built in 1860. Its funnel-shaped smokestack stopped sparks and cinders from flying out of the firebox. It prevented sparks from starting grass fires in the countryside over which the trains traveled.

The American Camelback locomotive, shown below, was introduced in 1900. The engineer's cab was built right on top of the boiler! This new type of engine burned coal instead of wood.

HOW A STEAM ENGINE WORKS

A steam engine produces power by combining fire and water to make steam. When steam builds up in a closed container, such as the boiler in a locomotive, it creates a lot of pressure. When that pressure is released, it is strong enough to move things such as the pistons and wheels of a steam engine. You can see how the steam engine in a locomotive works by looking at the diagram below.

(right) This train has stopped at a water tower to refill its boiler. Steam trains needed a lot of water to keep their engines running and had to stop many times to fill up.

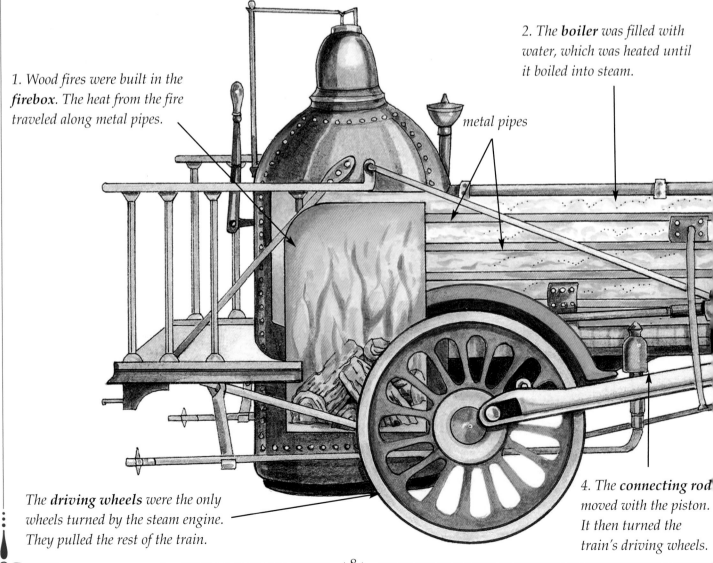

*1. Wood fires were built in the **firebox**. The heat from the fire traveled along metal pipes.*

*2. The **boiler** was filled with water, which was heated until it boiled into steam.*

metal pipes

*The **driving wheels** were the only wheels turned by the steam engine. They pulled the rest of the train.*

*4. The **connecting rod** moved with the piston. It then turned the train's driving wheels.*

The **smokestack** allowed smoke from the firebox to escape.

Making tracks

Mining companies used tracks long before the railroad was invented. Horses pulled carts full of **ore** out of the mines, but it was difficult for them to pull the carts over uneven ground. Miners laid strips of wood along the ground, and the ore carts ran on these makeshift rails. Railroad tracks were made of iron because iron is stronger than wood. Railroad builders also used **ties**, or squared-off logs, to support the tracks. They were placed underneath the rails to keep the tracks from sinking into the ground.

3. Steam from the boiler traveled into a **cylinder**. The pressure from the steam moved a **piston** back and forth inside the cylinder.

Truck wheels guided the locomotive along the tracks, helping the train turn safely and easily.

BUILDING A RAILROAD

The idea of a steam-powered locomotive caught the attention of many business people who had dreams of setting up **profitable** railroad companies in eastern North America. Building a railroad, however, with miles of tracks and expensive trains, required a lot of money. Companies found **investors**, or people who would provide money to start the work. The government also provided land and money.

East, then west

The first railroads were built in the East and linked large cities together. They were a great success, and soon the construction of the railroads turned west. Railroad companies started planning to build a railway across the continent. This **transcontinental** track would link the East and West and strengthen the United States and Canada as countries.

Choosing a route

Before companies began building, teams of men called **surveyors** explored the land to find the best places to lay track. This was not an easy task! The surveyors traveled through untouched wilderness, climbed up rocky cliffs, hiked through dense forests, and crossed turbulent rivers. They encountered all kinds of weather.

Laying the tracks

After the route was chosen, it was time to start construction. Supplies and crews of workers were taken by train to the end of the tracks. **Graders** prepared the ground by making the land **level**, or flat. Other workers laid the ties. The heavy iron rails were lifted into place and secured with long, metal spikes.

The lengths of iron rail were so heavy that it took three or four workers to lift each one.

Back-breaking work

Railroad companies wanted the track to be laid quickly, so construction was hectic. Supervisors shouted orders from galloping horses, and workers ran back and forth between the carts and the tracks carrying ties and rails. Others swung sledgehammers hard and fast, driving the metal spikes into the ground.

A fast pace

The swift pace meant that the crews usually finished three to five miles (5 to 8 kilometers) of track in a day. Ten miles (16 kilometers) in one day was considered a record! On difficult ground, however, a crew might only get as far as 70 feet (21 meters)! It took about five years to build the transcontinental line.

More than just tracks!

Many obstacles stood in the way of building a railway line. Steep hills could cause a train to barrel down the tracks at great speeds. To avoid sending a train out of control down a slope, the workers built the track in S-shaped curves. It took extra time and effort to build a winding track. Huge mountain ranges such as the Rockies and Sierra Nevadas presented an even bigger challenge! Dynamite was used to blast tunnels through the rock to make way for the railway tracks.

*(right) Blizzards or avalanches could bury the tracks in snow. Workers had to dig out the train and supplies! Sometimes they built **snow shelters** to cover the tracks and keep them clear of snow.*

(below) Building bridges was another enormous challenge for work crews!

Historic North American railroads

Some of the major railroad companies of the United States were the Northern Pacific, Great Northern, Central Pacific, Union Pacific, and Southern Pacific railways. The major Canadian companies were the Canadian Pacific Railway (CPR), and the Canadian National Railway (CNR).

The Canadian Pacific Railway built Canada's first sea-to-sea line. The last spike was driven in British Columbia in 1885. The event, shown on the right, was celebrated all across the country.

The Union Pacific and Central Pacific together completed America's first transcontinental railway line. One company set out from the East and the other from the West. In 1869, the last spike was driven at Promontory, Utah, shown below, where the two tracks met.

THE PEOPLE WHO BUILT THE RAILROAD

Railroad companies needed thousands of workers to build a transcontinental line. People from all over the world joined the railway-building crews. **Immigrants** from Ireland, Germany, Mexico, and China came to work on the railroads. Some Native Americans worked for the railway companies in the early days of building the railroad, but later disputes over the land made cooperation impossible.

Lonely times

The crews spent long days doing difficult, physical work. Many immigrants who came in search of a job could not afford to bring their families with them. Other workers did not want their families to live in the harsh, unsettled West. Many workers who left their wives and children behind did not see them for months at a time.

Conflicting cultures

Workers from other countries often did not speak English and had customs that were different from those of the North American workers. Many North American workers were unfamiliar with the cultures of the immigrants and held strong **prejudices** against them. A prejudice is a negative opinion based on race, religion, or gender. Immigrant workers were often given the most difficult and dangerous jobs because of prejudice.

Trains and towns

Railroad employees lived on **work trains** that followed the workers as they laid new track. The crews ate and slept on the work train. The **bunkhouse car**, where the workers slept, was cramped and dirty. If a railroad crew was expected to spend a long time working in one area, the workers built a small town, where they had larger, more comfortable places to live. Most of these "railroad towns" were not permanent, however. They were taken apart as soon as the work in that area was finished. The towns were set up again at the next work site.

This picture shows a work train with its railroad crew members and their families. On a typical work train, the first car behind the locomotive carried tools, supplies, and a blacksmith shop. The sleeping and dining cars came next. The last car on the work train served as a kitchen, store room, and the engineer's office.

People were excited about the invention of a new form of transportation. Many wanted to ride on the "iron horse." When trains began running, eager customers lined up to buy tickets. The price of the tickets depended on the distance and the level of luxury one required. The train was by far the easiest and fastest way to travel long distances!

A car for everything

Early railroad cars were wooden wagons with iron wheels. The first trains carrying people looked like stagecoach cars, as shown above. As time went on, however, new and better designs for train cars were developed. Later trains had many different kinds of cars, depending on their use.

Passenger trains carried people. Their **coaches**, or cars, had seats, tables, beds, and a kitchen for preparing food. **Freight trains** carried goods such as oil, grain, cattle, dry goods, and mail. The cars were designed to suit the cargo they carried. **Cattle cars** held horses and cattle and had holes in the sides to let in air. **Boxcars** held items such as coal or dry goods. They were plain, closed rectangles. **Flatcars** had no walls or roof. Large or bulky items such as machinery were chained down on the open platforms. **Tanker cars** were shaped like large cylinders and held liquids such as oil or water. **Mail cars** were spacious and well-lit, so postal workers could sort the mail as the train moved.

The tail end

The **caboose**, shown above, was located at the very end of the train. It served as an office, a place to sleep, and a lookout. While the train was moving, someone always stayed in the caboose to watch over the rest of the train. The caboose was usually painted red to signal that it was the end of the train.

A coach for everyone

Travelers on the railroad could buy tickets for one of three types of passenger cars. A first-class ticket was the most expensive. Second- and third-class tickets were more affordable.

Long-distance travelers

Many immigrants sailed across the ocean to North America. They traveled in crowded ships and arrived tired and sick. After their long sea voyage, they took the train to their new home in the West. Most immigrants traveled third class, but even that was a dream compared to traveling by boat or wagon train!

Third-class travel

A third-class ticket was the least expensive ticket available. Many people who traveled long distances to settle in the West chose third class because it was all they could afford. Third class had no dining or sleeping cars. Passengers had to bring food with them, and they slept in their seats or in hard bunks above the seats. Children played in the aisles, and pets roamed free.

Third class was the least comfortable of all the passenger cars. The wooden seats were rarely padded. Third-class coaches also tended to be crowded and noisy.

An affordable option

Second class was more comfortable than third class. Cushioned seats were shared by only two people. Meals, however, were not served to second-class travelers. If passengers did not bring their own food, they had to get off the train and buy a meal from a restaurant while the train refueled at a station.

(left) A young woman brushes her hair in the bathroom before going to bed. First- and second-class passengers could pay extra for a small room in a separate sleeping car. Others slept in their seats or in bunks.

Traveling in luxury

A first-class ticket was expensive, but it was worth it! First-class coaches were beautiful and comfortable. They had large, well-padded seats. In some coaches, travelers had a chair to themselves! For an extra fee, a seat that could be converted into a bed was available. Other trains had separate sleeping cars where travelers could rest comfortably on private beds with fresh linen.

Delicious meals and fine service

Meals were provided in a separate dining car. The tables were covered with white linen and set with fine china and silver. The meals were as elegant and delicious as those served at an expensive hotel or restaurant. The passengers were given excellent service as well. For those who could afford it, a first-class train ride was an adventure with all the comforts of home.

RAILWAY EMPLOYEES

Stopping a train was not easy in the early days of the railroad. The "brakes" were located on top of the train!

Railroad companies provided jobs for many people. Once the tracks were laid, people were hired to operate the railways. There were many kinds of jobs available. Some people worked on the trains, and others worked at a station or repaired the tracks.

Different jobs

The **engineer** drove the train. The **fireman** worked in the locomotive, shoveling wood or coal into the firebox. This dusty, dirty job, shown above, required strong arms and a strong back. The **flagman** worked at the other end of the train in the caboose. If a train broke down, the flagman had to walk down the tracks and warn the next train of the danger ahead. His red flag or lantern was a signal to the next train to stop immediately.

Dangerous tasks

Brakemen climbed up on top of the train while the train was moving. Their job was to turn the **brake wheels**, which were located on top of each car. Turning these wheels stopped the train. It was important for the brakemen to turn all the brake wheels at the same time. Otherwise, some cars would stop before others, causing them to bump into each other or break their **couplings**. Couplings were devices that connected the cars.

Other workers

The **conductor** of a train took tickets, dealt with passengers, and supervised the rest of the train crew. **Baggagemen** loaded and unloaded the passengers' bags. **Guards** dealt with any troublemakers. The **station agent** had a very heavy workload. He was in charge of ticket sales, giving out train orders, and putting up signals. He was so busy that he had to live at the train station!

*When railway cars had to be added to or removed from a train, the **switchman** was the person who hitched or unhitched the couplings between the cars. Sometimes he had to work while the train was still moving! His job was very dangerous. Many switchmen were injured or killed.*

These baggagemen spent their day carrying heavy suitcases and trunks between the station and the trains. They also had to keep track of the stops at which each bag had to be unloaded.

SMALL AND LARGE STATIONS

Railroads were built quickly, and the first railway stations were set up in a hurry. An unused boxcar or passenger coach often served as a temporary station. Eventually, permanent buildings replaced these makeshift stations.

Building the station

Some stations were no more than a wooden shack with a platform. Others were larger and more elaborate. Each railroad company built its stations a little differently. A person could tell which company owned a station by the style of its trim, roof, and windows. Some stations belonged to more than one railroad company. These stations were called **union stations**.

(right) The train did not stop to pick up mail at towns without stations. Someone held up the mailbag, and a worker on the train grabbed it as the train rolled by.

Kinds of stations

There were different kinds of train stations. At **fueling stops**, the trains received coal, water, and orders from the station agent. Fueling stops were usually located in remote areas where there were long stretches of track between towns. **Way stations** had a small waiting room for travelers. They were found in smaller towns where few people got on or off the trains.

Divisional stations were built at key points along the rails, such as major cities. These stations were much larger than fueling stops or way stations. They had large waiting rooms, and some had a restaurant. Divisional stations provided trains with fuel, maintenance, and repairs. Crews working on the trains ended their shifts at these stations. Hundreds of passengers passed through a divisional station each day.

Passing hoops

If a station agent had to give orders to a train, he signaled it to slow down as it came into the station. The station agent tied the orders to a long-handled metal hoop and held it up in the air. As the train passed, the engineer reached a hand out the window. He put his arm through the hoop, grabbing it from the station agent's hand. After removing the orders, he tossed the hoop out the window onto the ground. If there were no orders, a train could go straight past the station. A train that went through without stopping was called a **highball**.

This divisional station serviced many trains. Passengers could change trains or get a meal at large stations such as this one.

PROBLEMS AND SOLUTIONS

Railroads became widely used by passengers and by companies that transported goods. Several trains ran in different directions at all times of the night and day. Accidents often occurred because trains traveled towards each other on the same track. Wagons crossing the tracks and broken-down trains also caused accidents. Bad weather often posed problems. Sections of track were washed out by heavy rain, causing trains to **derail**, or go off the tracks. Railway companies had to find ways to make train travel safer!

Improved communication

In later days, station agents sent **telegraphs** to warn other stations of late trains or problems on the tracks. Telegraph messages were sent and received in **Morse code** over telegraph wires. Morse code is a series of long and short signals that represents letters of the alphabet. The pictures on page 25 show other warnings used to prevent accidents.

This station agent is decoding a message he received from another station by way of the telegraph transmitter. He can send a message by tapping out Morse code on the machine.

Flags were used during the day. The station agent used green, yellow, and red flags to signal whether a train was supposed to highball, slow down, or stop. Guess which colored flag gave each signal and explain your choices.

Train whistles were used as warning signs. The engineer pulled a cord, and a blast of steam from the engine escaped through the whistle. It made a piercing sound that could be heard for miles.

Small explosives called **torpedoes** were laid on the tracks to warn an engineer of danger ahead. A torpedo exploded when the train's wheels drove over it. If an engineer heard a torpedo, he knew he had to stop immediately.

Kerosene lamps hung from the front and back of the train. The lamps helped the engineer see the tracks and made the train visible to others.

Cowcatchers were attached to the front of locomotives. The cowcatcher prevented animals from getting caught under the wheels of the train, causing the train to crash.

Burning **flares** set near the tracks were also warnings. Red flares told engineers to stop, and yellow flares warned them to slow down.

Native Americans were the first people to live in North America. For thousands of years, they lived on the open land. When settlers first arrived in the West, the government signed a **treaty**, or agreement, stating that it owned certain areas of land, and Native Americans owned other areas.

Stolen land

When the transcontinental railroad was built, things began to change. Railroad companies planned to lay their track through Native American land. The government ignored the treaty and allowed the railway to be built on the Native land. The Native Americans were angry because their rights were ignored and they were being driven off their land.

The mighty buffalo

Many groups of Native Americans relied on the buffalo that roamed on the plains. They ate the meat, made tipis, clothing, and blankets from the skins, and fashioned tools out of the horns and bones. Native Americans used every part of the buffalo and killed only the animals they needed.

Changing a way of life

When the railroad was built, the buffalo began to scatter. Railroad workers and passengers shot the buffalo for sport from moving trains. They did not stop to collect the dead animals. Buffalo herds got smaller and smaller. The practice of killing buffalo for fun was wasteful, and it threatened the traditional Native American way of life. Native Americans needed the buffalo to survive. With their major source of food disappearing, many Native Americans faced starvation.

The fight for their rights

Native Americans decided that they had no choice but to fight against the building of the railroad. They tried everything to stop the railroad and save their land and culture. They destroyed tracks and derailed trains. They cut telegraph wires and fought railway workers. Eventually, the government sent troops to protect the railroad and the railway workers.

The end of the battle

Many Native Americans lost their lives in this struggle. The Native Nations realized they could not defeat the government or stop the progress of the railroad. They signed another treaty with the government. The government promised to set up **reservations** where Native Americans could live in peace. Although many reservations remain today, the traditional way of life of the Native American people was destroyed.

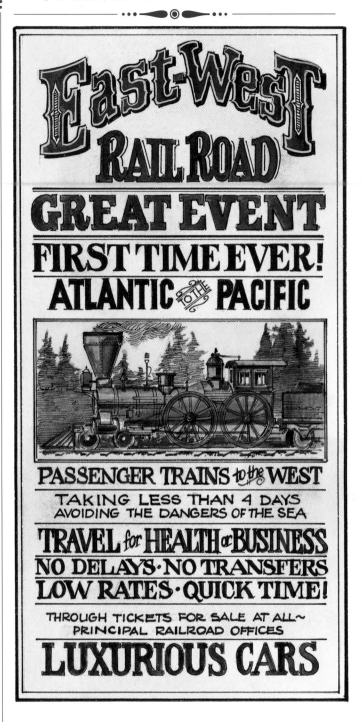

Railway stations and towns

More and more settlers were moving west. Towns began to appear in areas through which the railroad traveled. At first, many towns were centered around a railway station. The station was the most important place in the community. It often became a gathering place. Many parties, dances, and even weddings were held there! Some people found jobs at railway stations. Others set up businesses that sold goods to railway workers and passengers. Many of the workers and business owners also built homes near the stations. In time, isolated communities became busy towns.

Boomtowns

Railway stations caused towns to grow. Some railway towns became prosperous so quickly that their population doubled or tripled almost overnight! This sudden growth was called a **boom**, and the communities that experienced it became known as **boomtowns**.

Improving trade

Settling the West involved more than just towns and people. The settlers needed food, supplies, and equipment. The railroad kept a steady stream of goods coming from the East. People in the West could also sell their goods to the people who lived in the East.

New technology

As a business, the railroad was a great success and quickly became a booming industry that changed North America. Railroad companies made money, and companies that used the railroad to transport goods also made money. It was the beginning of a time when machines began to replace human and animal labor.

The Industrial Revolution

The change from human labor to machines was called the **Industrial Revolution**. Using machines, factories were able to make products quickly and inexpensively. People no longer made cloth and clothes by hand. They could buy them in shops or order them from catalogs. It often took an artisan months to make a table, but a factory could make furniture in a matter of hours. Machine-made goods cost less money because machines did much of the work and did not have to be paid.

More money to spend

People worked in factories and earned money to buy goods. Earning and spending money became a new way of life, made possible by the railroad. It moved people and goods from place to place quickly, helping businesses to succeed.

The effect of the railroad

Railroads were a major step in the development of the United States and Canada. Without them, it would have taken people months to reach the West, and many would not have undertaken the difficult journey. The transcontinental lines brought settlers to the West, populating North America from coast to coast. The railroads also brought thousands of immigrants from other countries. These newcomers settled much of the West, bringing with them the cultures and traditions that are now a part of North America's rich multicultural heritage.

Glossary

boomtown A town that grows quickly in population and wealth

cowcatcher A triangular grid on the front of a locomotive used to prevent animals from getting caught under the train

emigrate To leave one's home for the purpose of living in another place

highball A train that passes through a station without stopping

immigrant A person who comes to live in a place that is far from where he or she was born

investor A person who gives money to a business or project

last spike The event in the United States and Canada that marked the completion of the transcontinental railroads

ore Mineral or rock that is mined for the metal it contains

reservation An area of land set aside by the government on which Native Americans live

snow shelter A wooden structure built over railroad tracks to prevent snow from piling up on the tracks

station agent The person in charge of managing a railway station

steam engine A motor that is powered by steam

telegraph A machine that sends and receives electronic signals

transcontinental Describing something that crosses a continent

treaty An agreement between governments or nations, usually written at the end of a battle or war

wagon train A group of covered wagons in which many settlers traveled west

INDEX

ACKNOWLEDGMENTS

Photographs and reproductions:
Jakob Gogolin, Kansas State Historical Society (detail): page 27
Mark Horn: page 4
Image Club Graphics: page 26 (top)
Kansas State Historical Society: pages 8, 11, 14 (top), 18 (both), 21, 22, 30–31
Library of Congress: pages 5, 16, 24
Minnesota Historical Society: page 15
Montana Historical Society, Helena: pages 12 (bottom), 14 (bottom)
Frances Flora Bond Palmer, *Across the Continent.* *"Westward the Course of Empire Takes Its Way."* lithograph, 1868, Amon Carter Museum, Fort Worth, Texas (detail): pages 28–29

Tony and Alba Sanches-Zinnanti: pages 9, 20 (top)
Western Canada Pictorial Index: pages 12 (top), 13 (top), 20 (bottom)
Wyoming Division of Cultural Resources: pages 13 (bottom), 23

Illustrations and colorizations:
Barbara Bedell: cover, title page, pages 6–7, 8–9, 17, 19, 22, 23, 24, 25, 26 (bottom)
Bonna Rouse: pages 10–11, 15, 16, 21, 28 (left)